More Heavenly Cakes

Recipes from the Dorchester Abbey Tea Room

Compiled by Ann Wells and Steph Forman

Parochial Church Council of the Abbey Church
of St Peter and St Paul
Dorchester-on-Thames, Oxfordshire

Sold in aid of Dorchester Abbey

Customers enjoying tea in the Tea Room Courtyard

*First published in 2019 by the Parochial Church Council
of the Abbey Church of St Peter and St Paul,
Dorchester-on-Thames, Oxfordshire, OX10 7HZ
www.dorchester-abbey.org.uk
Compiled by Ann Wells and Steph Forman*

*Photographs: Nigel Gibson, Frank Blackwell, Steph Forman, John
Metcalfe, Nick Forman*

ISBN 978-0-9545435-4-9

Contents

Introduction

On Easter Saturday every year, Dorchester reopens its Abbey Tea Room to a hungry crowd of villagers and regulars keen to be sharing excellent home made cake served in the lovely surroundings of our ancient Abbey Guest House. The communal tables groan with lemon drizzle and coffee cake and this week's 'special' and new friends are made across pots of tea. In the sunny courtyard families and walkers collect trays from the hatch and enjoy a well earned treat under sun umbrellas.

This perfect slice of village life continues the hospitality of the Augustinian monks of Dorchester Abbey, who provided food and drink to monastery visitors in medieval times. In 1977 Lettice Godfrey, a retired teacher, rekindled this tradition and started to serve morning coffee and biscuits, gradually growing the enterprise into the Tea Room you see today. Lettice was awarded the BEM for her work at the Tea Room and other services to the community. By the time she hung up her apron in 1999 it had featured in many well known guides, achieved glowing media reviews and had repeat visitors from California to the Australian outback.

Our current Tea Room is still completely staffed and caked by enthusiastic volunteers—around 100 of them! It raised over £18,000 last year and over half of that money is donated to charity by the Abbey.

More Heavenly Cakes brings *Heavenly Cakes* up to date with new recipes from our current bakers and keeps a good selection of the traditional favourites. Our bakers' recipes are based on sources from family to internet and social media or the latest celebrity cookbooks, with small changes made by the baker based on their experience. Many of these cakes are tea room regulars, appearing week after week, often gone to early customers within the first hour of opening.

We hope that you will enjoy baking from our book and thank you for buying it and contributing to the upkeep of Dorchester Abbey. But do continue to support our Tea Room!

Steph Forman
Tea Room Coordinator

The Abbey Tea Room helpers 1981 (Lettice seated to the right of the board)

Scones and
Tea Breads

Scones

Margot Metcalfe

This is the basic recipe used every weekend – about 3 dozen are consumed each day, either plain or with jam and cream.

INGREDIENTS
(Makes 36 small scones)
700g self-raising flour
125g soft margarine
125g caster sugar
pinch of salt
425ml milk
milk to glaze
(add raisins if you wish)

PREPARATION
Grease two baking trays
Heat oven to 225°C/Fan 210°C/Gas 7-8

METHOD
1. Sift the flour into large mixing bowl.
2. Rub the flour and margarine together, or use a pastry cutter, until texture resembles fine breadcrumbs.
3. Mix in the sugar and salt.
4. Add milk until the dough is firm but not sticky.
5. Add raisins here if you wish!
6. Roll out the dough to 1 cm thick on a floured surface
7. Cut out as many scones as possible with a floured 4.5cm cutter.
8. Place on a baking sheet and brush with milk.
9. Bake for about 15 minutes or until golden brown.

Savoury Cheese Scones

Judy Parker

INGREDIENTS
(Makes 12 small scones)
225g self-raising flour
pinch of salt
pinch cayenne pepper
175g grated Cheddar cheese
115g butter
1 small egg (beaten)
scant 115ml water

PREPARATION
Grease a baking tray
Heat oven to 220°C/Fan 200°C/Gas 7

METHOD
1. Rub the flour, salt, cayenne and butter together until the mixture resembles coarse breadcrumbs
2. Stir in the grated cheese.
3. Add enough water to make a firm, pliable dough.
4. Pat out the smooth dough to 1 cm (½ inch) thick.
5. Cut out with a floured cutter or knife.
6. Brush with beaten egg and sprinkle with a little extra grated cheese.
7. Bake for about 15-20 minutes until golden brown.
8. Serve warm.

Banana Nut Bread

Rene Hender

INGREDIENTS
175g self-raising flour
½ level tsp salt
1 level tsp mixed spice
115g caster sugar
40g chopped walnuts
2 medium-sized ripe bananas
1 large egg
25g butter, melted

PREPARATION
Grease and line a 900g loaf tin
Heat oven to 180°C/Fan 160°C/Gas 4

METHOD
1. Sift the flour, salt and mixed spice into a mixing bowl.
2. Stir in the sugar and walnuts.
3. Peel the bananas and mash to a puree with a fork.
4. Add to the dry ingredients along with the egg and melted butter.
5. Stir to blend the ingredients, then beat thoroughly to mix.
6. Spoon the mixture into the tin and spread evenly.
7. Bake for 1 hour.
8. Turn out and leave until cold.
9. Serve sliced and buttered.

Fruity Earl Grey Tea Loaf

Meg Fisher

A Wednesday team regular cake which tastes amazing simply buttered!

INGREDIENTS
2 earl grey tea bags
250g dried mixed fruit
60g dark brown muscovado sugar
275g plain flour
2½ tsp baking powder
1tsp ground mixed spice
¼ tsp salt
2 oranges, I finely grated for zest
2 large eggs
50g granulated sugar

PREPARATION
Grease and line a 900g loaf tin
Heat oven to 180°C/Fan 160°C/Gas 4

METHOD
1. Place the tea bags in a medium saucepan and pour over 300ml boiling water. Simmer for 2 mins then take out the tea bags.
2. Stir in the fruit and muscovado sugar and simmer for another minute then transfer to a large mixing bowl.
3. Stir together the flour, baking powder, spice, salt and grated orange zest.
4. Stir the eggs into the cooling tea mix followed by the dry ingredients.
5. Spoon into the tin and bake for 1 hour.
6. 20mins before the end of baking pare the rind of the other orange and cut into thin strips. Heat 25g of the granulated sugar in a small saucepan with the juice of ½ the orange, stir until dissolved.
7. Add the orange strips, leave to cool slightly then stir in the remaining sugar. Spoon over the cake while still warm in the tin then leave to cool.

Apricot and Nutmeg Loaf

Anne Alcock

INGREDIENTS
175g self-raising flour
pinch of salt
½ teaspoon ground nutmeg
80g butter
80g demerara sugar
115g dried apricots
2 level tablespoons golden syrup
2 tablespoons milk
2 eggs

PREPARATION
Well grease and flour a 450g loaf tin
Heat oven to 190°C/Fan 170°C/Gas 5

METHOD
1. Cut the dried apricots into small pieces.
2. Sift together flour, salt and nutmeg and rub in the butter.
3. Add sugar and apricots.
4. In a separate bowl, blend together syrup, milk and eggs.
5. Lightly mix with dry ingredients.
6. Turn into the prepared tin.
7. Bake in the centre of the oven for about 1 hour (test with a sharp knife point which should emerge clean).
8. Cool for a few minutes then turn onto a wire rack.
9. To serve, slice and butter.

Specials

Fresh Cream and Strawberry Cake

Anne Parker

INGREDIENTS
4 medium fresh eggs
Weight of the eggs for: butter
caster sugar
self-raising flour
1 level tsp baking powder
½ tsp vanilla essence
A splash of milk if required
<u>Filling:</u> a punnet of strawberries
500 ml double cream
2 tbsp icing sugar, 3 tbsp strawberry jam, mint leaves

PREPARATION
Base line and grease 2x20cm sandwich tins
Heat oven to 180°C/Fan 160°C/Gas 4

METHOD
1. Cream the butter and sugar together until pale and fluffy.
2. Beat the eggs in a jug and slowly add to the mixture while beating.
3. Sieve the baking powder to the self-raising flour into the mixture with the vanilla essence, slowly fold in using a metal spoon
4. Add a little milk to reach dropping consistency.
5. Spoon the mixture equally into the 2 tins & bake for 25 to 30 mins until golden brown on top and firm when touched
6. Allow to cool in the tins.
7. Spread strawberry jam on the top of one cake .
8. Whisk up the double cream to soft peaks ,spoon half on top of the jam and spread evenly, place 2nd cake on top.
9. Sieve icing sugar over the top of the cake & pipe rosettes.
10. Place a strawberry on top of each rosette and finish off with mint leaves.

Ginger Lemon Drizzle Cake

Steph Forman
This delicious blend of ginger & lemon is a regular weekend favourite!

INGREDIENTS

Cake
140g butter, cut into cubes
300g self-raising flour
1 tsp bicarbonate of soda
4 tsp ground ginger
2 tsp mixed spice
1 tsp ground cinnamon
140g dark muscovado sugar
140g black treacle
140g golden syrup
300ml whole milk
1 large egg

Lemon drizzle
zest and juice 1 lemon
50g granulated sugar
50g preserving sugar

For the lemon curd filling
½ jar good lemon curd
2 balls stem ginger, diced

For the creamy filling
4 tbsp syrup from the ginger jar
75g soft cheese
150ml double cream
3 tbsp icing sugar, sieved

PREPARATION
Grease & line a 20cm round cake tin
Heat oven to 160°C/Fan 140°C/Gas 3

METHOD
1. Put the flour, bicarbonate of soda and all the spices into a food processor, add the butter and whizz, then tip into a mixing bowl.
2. Put the sugar, treacle, golden syrup and milk in a saucepan and heat, stirring gently, until the sugar has dissolved. Turn up the heat and bring the mixture to just below boiling point.
3. Pour the treacle mixture into the dry ingredients, stirring with a wooden spoon as you go. Beat in the egg until the mixture resembles a thick pancake batter. Pour into the prepared tin and bake for 50 mins-1 hr, until a skewer poked in the centre comes out clean. Leave to cool completely in the tin.
4. Split the cake through the middle.
5. For the filling, mix the lemon curd with the diced ginger. For the creamy filling, beat together the ginger syrup, soft cheese, cream and icing sugar until thick enough to hold its shape.
6. Spread the lemon curd filling all over the cut side of the bottom cake, dollop the creamy filling on top, then sandwich.
7. Stir the drizzle ingredients together then spoon over the cake top.

Raspberry & White Chocolate Ripple Cake

Steph Forman

INGREDIENTS

Cake
4 eggs
Egg weight of:
  self-raising flour (sieved)
  caster sugar
  butter (at room temp)
1½ tsp baking powder
1 tbsp milk
100g raspberry jam

Icing
50g white chocolate
150g granulated sugar
3 large egg whites
270g unsalted butter
80g seedless raspberry jam

PREPARATION

Base line and grease 2 x 20cm round cake tins
Heat oven to 180°C/Fan 160°C/Gas 4

METHOD

1. Put the eggs, flour, caster sugar, butter, baking powder and milk into a bowl and mix until thoroughly combined.
2. Pour the cake mixture into the tins and bake in the oven for 25mins or until a skewer inserted into the centre comes out clean.
3. Leave to cool for 10mins in the tins and then cool on a rack.
4. Melt the chocolate in a microwave for 1 min & stir until smooth.
5. Put 100ml of water with the sugar into a pan over a medium heat and stir until the sugar is dissolved. Bring to the boil.
6. Put the egg whites into a clean bowl and whisk until stiff. When the syrup reaches 121C, pour it down the side of the bowl with the whisk still running. Whisk on high speed until the bowl has cooled.
7. With the mixture on medium, gradually add the butter until fully combined. Split the icing into the two bowls, adding the white chocolate to one and half the jam to the other.
8. Split both cakes in half and start to assemble the cake.
9. Lay the top of one of the cakes face down and cover with white chocolate icing. Place another layer on it and cover with raspberry jam. Cover with another layer and chocolate icing and then finally put the top layer on and cover the whole cake with raspberry icing, randomly swirling in any left over chocolate icing and jam.

Strawberry & Elderflower Cake

Felicity Burrell

INGREDIENTS

<u>Cake</u>
175g caster sugar
175g butter
175g self-raising flour
3 eggs

<u>Filling</u>
125g soft butter
250g icing sugar
2 tbsp elderflower cordial
200g strawberries
1 tbsp sugar
Splash balsamic vinegar

PREPARATION
Base line and grease 2 x 20cm round cake tins
Heat oven to 180°C/Fan 160°C/Gas 4

METHOD
1. Beat butter and sugar together until light and fluffy.
2. Add eggs one at a time with 1tsp of the flour, beating between each egg, then fold in the rest of the flour.
3. Divide between the two tins and bake for 20 to 30 mins until risen and springy.
4. Leave the cakes to cool in the tins for 5 mins then turn out onto a wire rack.
5. Whip the softened butter with the icing sugar and cordial.
6. Chop the strawberries and heat with the sugar and balsamic vinegar, mix in the jam and cool.
7. Layer the cake with the fillings.
8. Dust the top of the cake with icing sugar.

Death by Chocolate (or Coffee)

Coffee Cake

Susan Jupp

This is the most popular coffee cake we sell, always available at weekends and often sold out.

INGREDIENTS

Cake	Filling and Topping
3 large eggs (at room temp)	85g butter at room temp
Equal weight of the eggs of:	170g icing sugar
Butter at room temp	1 tbsp Camp Coffee
Caster sugar	
Self-raising flour	
1 tbsp Camp Coffee	

PREPARATION

Grease & line 2 x 20cm sandwich tins
Preheat oven to 180°C/Fan 160°C/Gas mark 6

METHOD

1. Crack the eggs into a jug and leave to one side. Beat the butter, caster sugar and camp coffee until creamy, add the eggs one at a time with a spoon of the flour, beating the mixture each time until the mixture looks creamy again.
2. Sift the remaining flour onto the mixture and fold in with 1 tbsp of hot water.
3. Spoon the mixture into the cake tins and smooth down.
4. Bake in the preheated oven for 25 to 30 minutes.
5. Leave in the tins for five minutes, then carefully tip out to cool on the cooling rack.
6. Beat the icing sugar, butter and camp coffee until well blended.
7. When the cakes are cold, sandwich them together using half the butter icing, and spread the rest of the butter icing onto the top of the cake.

Cappuccino cake

Jilly Cook

It's difficult to beat this classic combination of coffee and chocolate. This cake is best eaten fresh but that's not something we've ever had a problem with!

INGREDIENTS

Cake
50g cocoa powder
6 tbsp boiling water
3 large eggs
60ml milk
175g self-raising flour
1 rounded tsp baking powder
100g butter at room temp
275g caster sugar

Filling and Topping
300ml double cream
1 tsp instant coffee, dissolved in 2 tsp hot water
A little cocoa powder for dusting

PREPARATION
Grease 2 x 20 cm sandwich tins 4cm deep
Heat oven to 180°C/Fan 160°/Gas 4

METHOD
1. Mix the cocoa powder with the boiling water in a large mixing bowl
2. Add all the remaining ingredients and whisk until just combined to a thick batter. (Do not overwhisk)
3. Divide the cake mixture between the prepared tins and gently level the surface, Bake for 25-30mins until well risen and beginning to shrink away from the sides of the tins. Turn onto a wire rack and leave to cool completely
4. To finish the cake, whip the cream until it holds it shape and then stir in the dissolved coffee. Use half the cream to fill the cake and spread the remainder over the top. Gently smooth the surface with a palette knife and dust with sifted cocoa.
5. Best eaten fresh!

Chocolate Cake

Linda Oliver

INGREDIENTS
Cake
150g self-raising flour
25g cocoa (sieved with flour)
175g butter
175g caster sugar
3 free-range eggs
1 tsp baking powder
1 tbsp warm water
Icing
40g butter
25g cocoa (sieved)
115g icing sugar (sieved)
2-3 tbsp milk

PREPARATION
Grease 2 x 20 cm sandwich tins
Heat oven to 180°C/Fan 160°C/Gas 4

METHOD
1. Put all ingredients in a food processor
2. Process for 10-15 seconds until mixture is well beaten
3. Divide between tins
4. Bake for 10-15 minutes until risen and springy
5. Remove from oven and leave to cool slightly
6. Turn out on cooling rack
7. For icing, first melt butter in small pan over a medium heat.
8. Take the pan off the heat and add the milk. Stir to blend, then add icing sugar and cocoa and beat well until mixture is blended and slightly thickened.
9. Place half the mixture on one cake, place the second cake on top, and spread the remaining icing over the top.

Chocolate Brownies

Steph Forman

A simple brownie recipe which takes minutes to make, doesn't need a mixer, and always gets rave reviews. The more it wobbles when you take it out the fudgier your brownies are—your choice!

INGREDIENTS
375g dark chocolate, broken into pieces
375g butter
6 eggs
500g caster sugar
1 tsp vanilla extract
225g plain flour
1 tsp salt
Chocolate chips (about half a bag)

PREPARATION
Line a 23cm x 30cm baking tin
Heat oven to 200°C/Fan 180°C/Gas 5

METHOD
1. Melt the chocolate and butter on high in the microwave for 3mins, stirring halfway through.
2. Beat the eggs, sugar and vanilla together.
3. Mix the melted chocolate, flour and salt into the eggs and sugar.
4. Pour into the tin.
5. Sprinkle with chocolate chips.
6. Bake for 40mins or until it stops wobbling.
7. Leave to cool into the tin. Cut into squares.

Oranges
Lemons &
Limes

Lime & Coconut Drizzle Loaf

Linda Oliver

INGREDIENTS
Cake
175g self-raising flour
1 level tsp baking powder
pinch of salt
175g butter, diced
175g golden caster sugar
3 medium eggs, beaten
50g desiccated coconut
zest and juice of 2 limes
Icing
1 lime
115g sifted icing sugar
1 tbsp sweetened and tenderised coconut

PREPARATION
Grease and line a a 900g loaf tin
Heat oven to 180°C/Fan 160°C/Gas 4

METHOD
1. Put all the cake ingredients into a large bowl.
2. Mix with a free-standing beater until well-mixed.
3. Pour the mixture into the tin.
4. Bake for 45-55 minutes until golden and a skewer inserted into the middle comes out clean.
5. Leave to cool for 10 minutes.
6. Lift or turn out the cake, keeping it in the liner if used.
7. For icing, finely grate the zest from the lime and squeeze the juice, add the icing sugar and blend until smooth. Pour over the cake, and sprinkle the coconut on top .

Orange and Ginger Cake

Susan Jupp

INGREDIENTS

Cake
200g butter
200g caster sugar
4 large eggs
grated rind of 2 large oranges
200g self-raising flour
1 heaped tsp ground ginger

Orange and ginger crust
Grated rind and juice of 1 orange
80g granulated sugar
2 pieces of preserved ginger, finely chopped

PREPARATION
Grease a 23 cm spring form tin and line base
Heat oven to 180°C/Fan 160°C/Gas 4

METHOD
1. Beat the butter well.
2. Gradually add sugar and beat until the mixture is pale and fluffy.
3. Beat in one egg and the grated orange rind.
4. Beat in the flour and ginger, sieved together, alternating with the other three eggs to avoid curdling of the mixture.
5. Put into the prepared tin.
6. Bake for 35-40 minutes, until it springs back when lightly pressed in the centre with your finger.
7. Meanwhile, for the topping, mix together the orange rind and juice, sugar and chopped ginger.
8. Remove the cake from oven.
9. While still hot prick the top in several places with a skewer.
10. Spoon the topping over the surface.
11. Leave cake in tin until cool.

This cake is adapted from the recipe in Claire McDonald of McDonald's' 'Celebrations' recipe book.

Lemon Cream Sponge

Beth Lynch-Blosse

INGREDIENTS

Cake	Filling
3 medium eggs	Juice of ½ lemon
Egg weight of:	50g unsalted butter
self-raising flour + 25g	115g icing sugar
butter	
granulated sugar	Icing
rind of one medium lemon, grated	Juice of ½ lemon
	115g icing sugar

PREPARATION
Grease 2 x 19 cm sandwich tins
Heat oven to 180°C/Fan 160°C/Gas 4

METHOD
1. Mix all cake ingredients together in bowl with an electric beater, or in an electric cake mixer.
2. Put into tins.
3. Bake for 20-25 minutes.
4. Let the cakes cool until quite cold.
5. For filling, beat together the lemon juice, butter and icing sugar and spread over one half of the cake. Cover with the other half.
6. For icing, mix lemon juice with icing sugar to make a fairly stiff coating and spread over the top of the cake.

Lemon Drizzle Cake

'Jonesy'

This cake was a speciality of the late Elsie Jones, better known as 'Jonesy', and appeared regularly on Saturdays.

INGREDIENTS
<u>Cake</u>
225g plain flour
2 teaspoons baking powder
225g sugar
4 eggs
225g margarine
zest of 1 lemon
tbsp icing sugar
juice of 1 lemon

PREPARATION
Base line and grease a 900g loaf tin
Heat oven to 180°C/Fan 160°C/Gas 4

METHOD
1. Mix all the cake ingredients together.
2. Put into a tin.
3. Bake for approximately 1 hour.
4. Leave in the tin until cold.
5. Pierce the top and sides of cake with a skewer.
6. Mix the syrup ingredients.
7. Gradually spoon into holes (*'a bit tedious'*)
8. Add a bit of icing sugar to the last drop of syrup and spread over the top of the cake to give a crusty surface.

Fruits of
the Garden

Dorset Gooseberry Cake

Christiane Norman

In Lettice's day this used to be <u>the</u> weekly tea room favourite, and was always the first cake to go! It also makes a great pudding served hot with custard.

INGREDIENTS
225g self-raising flour
½ level tsp baking powder
115g mixed fats (half butter, half white fat)
¼ level tsp salt
225g prepared gooseberries or cooking apples
115g granulated sugar + extra sugar

PREPARATION
Grease, base line and re-grease an 18 cm sandwich tin
Heat oven to 175°C/Fan 155°C/Gas 3-4

METHOD
1. Halve gooseberries/chop prepared apples to size of sultanas.
2. Cover fruit with sugar on a large plate.
3. Sift the baking powder, salt and flour together.
4. Rub in the fats.
5. Mix the fruit into the flour.
6. Press into the tin, ensuring the fruit does not touch the sides.
7. Bake for 1- 1¼ hours.
8. Turn out on to wire cooling tray and remove the lining paper.
9. Sprinkle with extra sugar
10. Serve with cream

Spicy Apple Cake

Anne Alcock

INGREDIENTS
175g butter
175g sugar
175g self-raising flour
¾ teaspoon mixed spice
3 eggs
2 apples

PREPARATION
Line a deep 18cm loose-bottomed sandwich tin
Heat oven to 175°C/Fan 155°C/Gas 3-4

METHOD
1. Peel, core and coarsely chop the apples.
2. Mix the flour and mixed spice.
3. Add all the ingredients except apples and mix together.
4. Stir in the apples
5. Bake for approximately 45 minutes (test when golden brown by inserting a knife point which should come out clean).
6. Allow to cool completely before turning out.
7. Can be served cold, or warm as a dessert with cream or ice-cream

Lemon & Elderflower Cake

Sandra Crawshaw

This is a wonderful moist summery cake and a weekly tea room favourite, best kept in the fridge.

INGREDIENTS
3 large eggs
200g caster sugar
3 tsp lemon extract
250ml elderflower cordial
250ml rapeseed oil
300g plain flour
3 tsp baking powder

250g icing sugar mixed with lemon juice

250ml of lemon juice
200g sugar
2 grated limes

PREPARATION
Base line and grease a 20cm cake tin
Heat oven to 180°C/Fan 160°C/Gas 4

METHOD
1. Beat the eggs, caster sugar & lemon extract until pale.
2. Beat in the rapeseed oil & elderflower cordial.
3. Fold in the flour and baking powder.
4. Pour into the cake tin.
5. Cook for 35 mins until golden and a skewer inserted into the middle comes out clean.
6. As soon as you take it out of the oven pour over the lemon juice mixed with the sugar.
7. Leave to cool.
8. Mix the icing sugar and lemon juice and pour over the cake, decorating with grated lime when set.

Fruit Streusel Cake

Mary Reaugh

Perfect for using up a glut of any fruit from the garden, blackcurrants or a mixture of berries or apples, plums or rhubarb all work well for this streusel recipe.

INGREDIENTS

Cake
175g self-raising flour, sifted
115g butter, room temp
115g caster sugar
2 eggs
½ tsp vanilla essence
1-2 tbsp milk
350g fruit, fresh or frozen
(thaw and dry)

Streusel Topping
60g self-raising flour
60g oatmeal
80g butter
80g caster sugar

PREPARATION
Grease a 22.5cm spring-clip tin
Heat oven to 180°C/Fan 160°C/Gas 4

METHOD
1. For the streusel topping, sift flour into a bowl, rub in butter until mixture resembles coarse crumbs, add sugar and set aside.
2. Cream the butter and sugar in a mixing bowl until soft and light.
3. Lightly mix the eggs and vanilla essence and add to the creamed mixture a little at a time, beating well after each addition and adding a little of the sifted flour with the last addition of egg
4. Gently fold in the flour and milk and mix until blended
5. Spoon the cake mixture into the prepared tin and spread level
6. Cover with the blackcurrants & sprinkle the topping evenly over the fruit
7. Bake for 1 hour and then allow to cool in the tin
8. Dust with icing sugar

Scandinavian Apple Cake

Jean Kestner

INGREDIENTS

Cake
350g self-raising flour
175g caster sugar
175g margarine
1 large egg
½ tsp vanilla essence
pinch of salt

Filling
2 large cooking apples
squeeze of lemon juice
2 tbsp caster sugar

Icing sugar to finish

PREPARATION
Line a loose-sided 23 cm tin with non-stick parchment
Heat oven to 180°C/Fan 160°C/Gas 4

METHOD
1. Peel, core and slice the apples fairly thinly and place in a microwaveable shallow flan dish.
2. Squeeze the lemon juice and scatter the sugar over the apples .
3. Par-cook in microwave oven at full heat for approx four minutes, stirring once.
4. Rub the margarine into the flour.
5. Add the sugar, salt and vanilla essence.
6. Blend in the egg to make a soft pastry (or blend all together in a food mixer)
7. Pat three-quarters of the mixture into the bottom of the prepared tin.

8.   Lift the apples with a slotted spoon and spread evenly on the base.
9.   Roll out the remaining pastry lightly to a strip about 23 x 10cm cut into 6 full-length strips and 4 half strips, and lay in a lattice pattern on top of the cake.
10. Bake for approximately 1 hour until pale golden.
11. Allow to cool slightly before removing from the tin.
12. To serve immediately, sift over the icing sugar while still warm and allow to stand for 10 minutes.

Can be eaten hot as a dessert or cold as a cake

If freezing, omit the icing sugar, remove from the freezer 1-2 hours before serving, recrisp in the oven for 30 minutes at 150°C and add icing sugar to the warm cake.

Carrot Cake

Carol Cornelius

INGREDIENTS

Cake
170g dark brown sugar
3 large eggs
200ml vegetable oil
125g self-raising flour
170g plain wholemeal flour
3 tsp baking powder
¾ tsp bicarbonate of soda
1½ tsp mixed spice
¾ tsp ground ginger
¾ tsp ground nutmeg
255g grated carrot
110g sultanas
1 peeled & grated apple
45 ml apple juice

Icing
100g butter at room temp
200g icing sugar
100g full fat cream cheese
1tsp vanilla extract

PREPARATION
Base line and grease a 22cm cake tin
Heat oven to 180°C/Fan 160°C/Gas 4

METHOD
1. Beat sugar and eggs until creamy. Gradually beat in the oil.
2. Mix flours, baking powder and bicarbonate of soda and spices. Mix into the egg mixture with the carrot, apple and sultanas.
3. Add apple juice to give consistency of thick batter.
4. Pour into cake tin. Bake for 1 hour to 1½ hours until skewer inserted into the centre of the cake comes out clean.
5. Cool in the tin for 10 minutes then remove cake from tin and leave to cool on a wire rack.
6. To make the icing beat butter and cream cheese together until smooth and creamy
7. Add vanilla and stir in icing sugar. Add more sugar if needed until icing is thick and spreadable.
8. Spread icing onto the cooled cake.

Gin-soaked Blackberry & Apple Crumble Squares

Steph Forman

INGREDIENTS

Fruit filling
200g blackberries
100ml sloe gin
500g cooking apples
2tsp cinnamon
1tsp nutmeg
1tsp vanilla
50g light brown sugar
1 tbsp cornflour

Crumble
200g light brown sugar
220g plain flour
1tsp baking powder
100g porridge oats
200g salted butter, melted
Flaked almonds, to top

Cream cheese filling
250g cream cheese
25g icing sugar
1 egg
1tsp vanilla
1tbsp lemon juice

PREPARATION
Grease and line a 20cm square cake tin
Heat oven to
    200°C/Fan 390°C/Gas 6

METHOD
1. Toss the blackberries in the gin and leave to soak for a few hours. Strain, keeping the gin.
2. Peel, core and dice the apples. Add to a saucepan with 50ml water, cinnamon, nutmeg, vanilla and sugar. Simmer for 5mins.
3. Combine the cornflour with 50ml water and add to the pan with the leftover gin, simmer and stir for another 5mins.
4. Mix together the crumble ingredients until you get a sandy consistency. Press ⅔ of the mixture onto the bottom of the tin.
5. Beat the cream cheese ingredients until fluffy and spoon over the crumble base.
6. Scatter over the blackberries, cover with the apple mixture and crumble over the remaining crumble mixture.
7. Bake for 20mins, scatter with almonds and bake for a further 10mins.
8. Leave to cool then refrigerate for a few hours before cutting into squares to serve.

Dundee Cake

Joan Blackwell

INGREDIENTS
225g self-raising flour
175g butter
175g soft brown sugar
3 eggs
425g mixed dried fruit
1 tsp mixed spice
split almonds for top (if required)

PREPARATION
Base line and grease a 20 cm cake tin
Heat oven to 130°C/Fan 140°C/Gas mark 2

METHOD
1. Beat butter and sugar until creamy.
2. Beat in the eggs one at a time with a little of the flour (to avoid curdling)
3. Add the remaining flour and mixed spice.
4. Add the fruit and mix in well.
5. Put the mixture into a prepared tin.
6. Level the top (add almonds if required).
7. Bake for about 2 hours, or until a wooden cocktail stick inserted into centre of cake comes out clean.

Sticky Gingerbread

Kathleen Joyner

INGREDIENTS
225g butter
225g soft brown sugar
225g black treacle
350g plain flour
2 eggs, beaten
1 tbsp ground ginger
2 tsp ground cinnamon
pinch of salt
1 tsp bicarbonate of soda
275ml milk, warmed

PREPARATION
Grease and line a 25cm square tin
Heat oven to 140°C/Fan 120°C/Gas 1-2

METHOD
1. Slowly melt together the treacle, sugar and butter, stirring all the time.
2. Remove from the heat and stir in the beaten eggs.
3. Sieve flour, salt, cinnamon and ginger and stir into the melted mixture.
4. Sieve bicarbonate of soda into a mixing bowl and add warmed milk.
5. Add the treacle mixture and stir well.
6. Pour into the prepared tin.
7. Bake for 1-1¼ hours (fan-assisted or gas oven), or 1¼-1½ hours (conventional oven).
8. It may be necessary to cover the surface of the cake with greaseproof paper after 1 hour to prevent over-baking.
9. Allow gingerbread to cool before removing from tin and greaseproof paper.
10. Store in an airtight tin or wrapped in foil until needed.

Seed Cake

Vera Baker

This recipe arrived with the message: This cake is guaranteed to remind elderly gentlemen of teas taken with ancient great-aunts!

INGREDIENTS
225g plain flour
1 tsp baking powder
115g butter
115g caster sugar
1 dsp caraway seeds
2 eggs
a little milk

PREPARATION
Base line and grease a 20 cm tin
Heat oven to 180°C/Fan 160°C/Gas mark 4

METHOD
1. Cream butter and sugar
2. Gradually add flour, baking powder, eggs, caraway seeds and a little milk
3. Turn into the tin and bake for 1½ hours
4. Leave to cool in the tin

Gentleman's Fruit Cake

Christiane Norman

A gentleman's fruit cake is a Dorchester village show category every autumn, and this is the recipe which was always shared with prospective entrants by the late Chris Norman. It's easy, reliable and absolutely delicious!

INGREDIENTS
500g mixed dried fruit
115g unsalted butter
255g granulated sugar
2 large eggs
240ml cold water
255g self-raising flour
1 tsp bicarbonate of soda
1 tsp mixed spice

PREPARATION
Grease a 20 cm cake tin and double line with foil
Heat oven to 160°C/Fan 140°C/Gas 3

METHOD
1. Put fruit, sugar, water, bicarbonate of soda & butter into a large saucepan. Bring to the boil & simmer for 15 mins on a low heat covered.
2. Leave to cool - overnight if possible.
3. Stir in the eggs, mix well then stir in flour sifted with spice and pour into tin.
4. Bake in pre-heated oven for approx. two hours. Cover the cake with a circle of greaseproof paper after an hour.
5. After 1 ½ hours reduce the temperature by 10°C.
6. Leave to cool for a short while and then turn out.

Almond Cake

Anne Alcock

INGREDIENTS
125g softened butter
25g plain flour
150g caster sugar
3 large eggs, beaten
75g ground almonds
finely grated rind of 1 lemon (optional)
demerara sugar

PREPARATION
Grease an 18cm sandwich tin
Heat oven to 180°C/Fan 160°C/Gas mark 4

METHOD

1. Beat the butter and caster sugar well with an electric whisk.
2. Whisk in small amounts of beaten egg and some ground almonds until all is well mixed.
3. Fold in the flour, remaining almonds and grated lemon rind with a metal spoon.
4. Pour into the sandwich tin and smooth the top.
5. Sprinkle with the demerara sugar.
6. Bake in the centre of the oven for 30-35 minutes.
7. Cool before turning out.

Date and Walnut Cake

Libby Vettewinkel

INGREDIENTS
225g block pressed dates, chopped
1 large lemon
50g chopped apricots
1 level tsp bicarbonate of soda
100g butter
100g soft brown sugar
1 egg
225g self-raising flour
100g broken walnuts
1 tbsp clear honey to glaze

PREPARATION
Lightly grease and base line a 20cm tin
Heat oven to 160°C/Fan 140°C/Gas mark 3

METHOD
1. Put the chopped dates, chopped apricots and finely grated lemon rind in a medium bowl.
2. Sprinkle with the bicarbonate of soda.
3. Squeeze the lemon juice and put in a measuring jug, make up to 225ml with boiling water and add to the bowl.
4. Stir well and leave until cold.
5. In a large bowl, beat butter and sugar together until smooth and creamy.
6. Stir the lightly beaten egg into the creamed mixture.
7. Stir in the date mixture.
8. Sift flour into the mixture
9. Stir until well mixed
10. Reserve about 25g of the broken walnuts and stir the remainder into the mixture
11. Spoon the mixture into the prepared tin, spread level and sprinkle with the reserved walnuts.

12. Bake for 1¼ hours.
13. Cool in the baking tin for 15 minutes, then turn onto a wire rack.
14. Brush the cake top with the warmed honey and leave until quite cold.

Flapjacks

Pam Reynolds

INGREDIENTS
150g butter
150g light brown soft brown sugar
225g porridge oats

PREPARATION
Grease and line a shallow 28cm x 18cm tin
Heat oven to 160°C/Fan 140°C /Gas 3

METHOD
1. Melt margarine and sugar in a pan over a low heat
2. Stir in the oats and mix thoroughly
3. Turn the mixture into the prepared tin
4. Bake for 10 minutes
5. Mark into 12 squares whilst still hot
6. Turn out when quite cold

'Health-giving' Oat Biscuits

Lettice Godfrey

These biscuits were a speciality of Lettice Godfrey, proprietress of the Tea Room 1977-1999, and promoted by her as the 'healthy option' for those not wishing to succumb to the temptation of a slice of cake!

INGREDIENTS
50g granulated sugar
115g margarine
150g porridge oats
25g lain flour
pinch of salt

PREPARATION
Flour a baking tray
Heat oven to 180°C/Fan 160°C/Gas 4

METHOD
1. Put all the ingredients into a large bowl.
2. Mix into one large pat.
3. Flour a board and pat the mixture down on it.
4. Roll out to about ½ cm thick.
5. Cut into shapes.
6. Place biscuits on a baking tray.
7. Bake until golden brown.
8. Let the biscuits cool a little, then place on a wire rack

Polenta Almond Lemon Drizzle cake
(Gluten Free)

Mary Reaugh

INGREDIENTS

Cake
200g unsalted butter
200g caster sugar
200g ground almonds
100g ground polenta
1½ tsp gluten free baking powder
3 large eggs
Zest of 2 lemons

Syrup
Juice of 2 lemons
125g icing sugar

PREPARATION
Base line and grease a 23cm springform tin
Heat oven to 180°C/Fan 160°C/Gas 4

METHOD
1. Cream the butter and sugar together until light pale and fluffy.
2. Mix together the almonds, polenta and baking powder and separately beat the eggs.
3. Alternate adding the dry ingredients and eggs and incorporate ¾ of the lemon zest.
4. Pour the mixture into the cake tin and bake in the centre of the oven for 40mins.
5. When the cake comes out of the oven prepare the syrup.
6. Combine the lemon juice, zest and icing sugar in a small saucepan and simmer until the sugar is dissolved.
7. While the cake is still warm and in the tin, prick it all over and then pour the syrup over the cake.
8. Leave in the tin until cold and then put straight onto a plate to serve.

Chocolate Ganache Cake
(Vegan)

Susanna Schenkel

INGREDIENTS

Cake
3 avocados, stoned and peeled
7 tbsp almond butter
8 tbsp cocoa powder
11 tbsp maple syrup
140g ground almonds
3 tbsp chia seeds

Icing
4 tbsp coconut oil
4 tbsp cocoa powder
4 tbsp maple syrup

PREPARATION
Base line and grease a 20cm round cake tin
Heat oven to 180°C/Fan 160°C/Gas 4

METHOD
1. Place all the cake ingredients into a food processor and blend until smooth.
2. Pour into the prepared tin and bake for 30mins until risen and golden brown.
3. Leave to cool in the tin for at least 20mins before turning out.
4. Make the icing: Warm the coconut oil in a pan until it melts.
5. Stir in the other ingredients in until you get a smooth glossy glaze.
6. Pour over the top of the cake and leave to set.

Orange and Almond Cake
(Gluten Free)
Steph Forman

This is a lovely moist cake that looks so pretty it's irresistible!

INGREDIENTS

Cake	Syrup
2 medium unwaxed oranges	4 Seville oranges or 4 ordinary
225g caster sugar	oranges and 1.5 lemons
1 tbsp honey	6 cardamom pods, lightly crushed
6 eggs, separated	1-3 tbsp caster sugar, to taste
300g ground almonds	2 tbsp candied orange peel
1/4 tsp salt	

PREPARATION
Base line and grease a 23cm springform tin
Heat oven to 180°C/Fan 160°C/Gas 4

METHOD
1. Put the oranges for the cake in a small pan and cover with water. Cover and bring to the boil, then turn down the heat and simmer for about 1.5-2 hours, turning once, until soft.
2. Drain and allow to cool slightly then cut open and remove any pips. Puree in a blender.
3. Beat together the egg yolks, sugar and honey until thick and pale, then fold in the almonds followed by the puree until well combined.
4. Whisk the egg whites and salt until stiff, then gradually fold into the batter, being careful to knock as little air out as possible.
5. Spoon into the tin and bake for about 45-50 minutes, or until firm on top.
6. Squeeze the fruit for the syrup into a pan and add the cardamom and a spoonful of sugar.

7. Bring to a simmer, stirring to dissolve the sugar, then taste and add more sugar as necessary.
8. Add the peel then allow to cool.
9. When the cake comes out of the oven, leave it in the tin and poke a few holes in the top with a skewer. Pour over the syrup a little at a time, and allow to sink in.
10. Serve either scattered with flaked almonds or drizzled with icing and decorated with candied peel.

Pear, Almond and Chocolate Cake
(Vegan & Gluten Free)

Steph Forman

It's great to have a vegan and gluten free cake that also looks indulgent and glamorous! This cake is best eaten fresh.

INGREDIENTS

For the dry mix:

290g white plain flour (can be gluten free)
75g ground almonds
3 teaspoons baking powder
¾ teaspoon baking soda
1 bar of vegan chocolate chopped up into chips
pinch of salt

For the wet mix:

275ml soy milk
1 1/2 tablespoon apple cider vinegar
130g coconut oil
170g brown sugar
120ml orange juice

3 large pears, peeled & cored.
Plain flour, 1tsp cinnamon
Melted chocolate to drizzle

PREPARATION

Base line and grease a 20cm springform tin
Heat oven to 180°C/Fan 160°C/Gas 4

METHOD

1. Chop 2 pears into pieces and 1 into slices (to decorate the top) & toss pieces and slices in flour with 1 tsp cinnamon.
2. Mix the dry ingredients in a large bowl.
3. In a small bowl combine soy milk and apple cider vinegar, let sit while you combine coconut oil, sugar and orange juice in a separate bowl. Add the soy and apple cider buttermilk.
4. Whisk together until everything is well combined.
5. Slowly add the wet mix to the dry mix and stir in the chopped pears. Take care not to overmix.
6. Place pear slices on top, sprinkle with almonds and bake for 45-50 minutes.
7. Remove from the oven and let cool before transferring to a serving plate. Drizzle with chocolate and serve.

Date, Banana & Rum Loaf
(Vegan & Gluten free)

Revd Sue Booys

INGREDIENTS
250g stoned dates
2 small / I large banana (140g approx.)
100g pecan nuts 85g chopped
200g raisins
200g sultanas
100g fine polenta
2 tsp mixed spice
2 tsp gluten free baking powder
3 tbsp dark rum (or orange juice)
4 tbsp aquafaba or egg replacement powder as product directs
(for non-vegan 2 egg whites may be used)
Banana chips and demerara sugar to decorate

PREPARATION
Grease and line a 2lb loaf tin
Heat oven to 180°C/Fan 160°C/Gas 4

METHOD
1. Put dates in a small pan with 200mls boiling water and simmer for 5 minutes.
2. Drain liquid into a jug.
3. Put the dates, banana and 100ml date liquid in food processor and whizz until smooth.
4. Mix chopped nuts, fruit, polenta, spice, and baking powder in a bowl. Add date puree and rum or orange juice and stir to combine.
5. Whisk aquafaba to stiff peaks (takes about 10 minutes in a stand mixer on high) and fold into the mixture.
6. Tip into tin and top with whole pecans, banana chips and sugar.
7. Bake for one hour. The top should be quite crusty and a skewer should come out clean.
8. Cool completely before slicing.

Beetroot Chocolate Cake
(Vegan)

Susanna Schenkel

INGREDIENTS

Cake
250g beetroot
400g buckwheat flour
360g apple puree
300ml maple syrup
6 tbsp cocoa powder
Pinch salt
Coconut oil for greasing

Icing
100g coconut cream
1 tbsp almond butter
2 tbsp maple syrup
1 tbsp cocoa powder

PREPARATION
Base line and grease a 25cm round cake tin
Heat oven to 190°C/Fan 170°C/Gas 5

METHOD
1. Steam the beetroot with the skin on until soft, about 1 hour, and then leave to cool. Peel.
2. Blend the beetroot to a smooth puree and then mix with all the other cake ingredients.
3. Pour into the cake tin and smooth the top.
4. Bake for 20mins

Make the icing:
5. Put the coconut cream into a bowl with 3 tbsp boiling water and stir until totally melted.
6. Put this into a blender with the almond butter, maple syrup and cocoa and blend until smooth.
7. Pour over the cake and leave to set.

Charities
Supported by
the Tea Room

THE NASIO TRUST VALUES
THE NASIO TRUST DERIVES ITS INSPIRATION AND VALUES FROM THE
FAITH AND BELIEVES THAT ALL PEOPLE ARE EQUAL AND ARE ENT
EQUAL OPPORTUNITY OR REGARDLESS OF THEIR SITUATION, FAITH
OR SOCIETY

The Nasio Trust

Charities Supported by the Tea Room

Tea Room profits are donated to a range of charities each year, with a number of regular donations and one-off donations.

A third of the donations are given to larger Anglican mission agencies supporting overseas projects. In addition an allocation is made towards emergency disaster appeals.

A third of the donations are made to charities where local individuals have a personal connection.

The final third is allocated to particular requests for support from Tea Room volunteers and members of the Abbey congregation.

In the last ten years alone we have supported over 80 charities including:

Church Mission Society
Oxford Asylum Welcome
Footsteps Foundation
Style Acre
Youth Challenge Oxford (YoCO)
Luther Street Medical Centre
Church Homeless Trust
Alzheimer's Society

Nasio Trust
Africare
PACT
Tuberous Sclerosis Association
Daybreak
Home Farm Trust
Oxford Community Soup Kitchen
Oxford Youth Works
Oxford WellChild Children's Nurse Appeal

Style Acre